Is Your Faith Ready for an Uplift?

Is Your Faith Ready For An Uplift?

Inspired by True Events in the Life of the Author

Kim Thompson

PALMETTO

P U B L I S H I N G

Charleston, SC

www.PalmettoPublishing.com

Scripture Quotations Taken from the King James Version of the Holy Bible, The New Living Translation©, English Standard Version, and the New International Version (NIV)

Paperback ISBN: 979-8-218-49145-1

Preface

Faith without works is dead. Most have read this scripture in James 2:26: "For as the body without the spirit is dead, so faith without works is dead also." If you have not read this scripture, please read it again in its context in James 2:14-26. A heart that has not been regenerated by God has empty professions; therefore, it is dead because it has no power. Now faith is the substance to things hoped for, and the evidence of things not seen (Hebrews 11:1). There is great power in the spoken word of faith. Jesus encourages us to articulate out loud and say what we are believing God for. Believing faith speaks. God's timing according to what you are believing for is perfect; He is never early or late because God is faithful and cannot lie. Hebrews 10:23 says, "Let us hold fast to the confession of our hope without wavering; for He is faithful that promised."

My prayer is for all of us to gain insightful knowledge to measure where our faith is and to take the time to analyze our faith so it will be pleasing unto God. If the development of our faith requires work, let us take action to enlarge it. Ask yourself these three questions: "Do I have faith?" "Do I want stronger faith?" Or, "Am I faithless?" My prayer: "Holy Spirit, I pray for your leading to help us develop the enlargement of our faith, which will defy explanations. In Jesus' name I pray, Amen."

Genesis 1:11- "And God said, Let the earth bring forth grass, the herb yielding seed, and the fruit tree yielding fruit after His kind, whose seed is upon the earth: and it was good." (KJV)

CONTENTS

Preface   v

1   Faith   1
2   How to Develop Faith   10
3   Do You Have Great or Little Faith?   19
4   Meditate on God's Word   26
5   Quintessential   34
6   The Voice of God   41
7   Psalm 37   52
8   Words   59
9   Living by Faith   67
10 Trials and Tribulations   76
11 Speaking the Word of God   84
12 Decree & Declare   92

    Acknowledgements/Contributions   101
    About the Author   103

1
Faith

So, you may ask the question, "Where does faith come from?" It is the instrument God uses to bring salvation to His people. He gives faith because of His grace and mercy and because He loves us. We are called to one Lord, one faith, one baptism, one God and Father of all, who is over all and through all, and in you all. (Ephesians 4:5-6). It comes to us in the form of a gift. God wants His people to know that this gift is not earned or to be boasted about. He gave it to us because of what He did on the cross for our salvation in Him. It is because Jesus lived a faithful life and died on the cross for us. If we get this concept twisted, we are truly thinking more highly than we ought.

"So then, faith cometh by hearing, and hearing by the Word of God" (Romans 10:17). Our faith is produced by reading the Bible, listening to a pastor preach, and through the experiences we encounter in our daily life, along with many other avenues. Faith also comes by people sharing the Word of God to others, by hearing sermons, listening to testimonials, hearing God's voice, or even by hearing the Word spoken through a vast number of other ways. There are many forms of perspectives and attention getters on awareness and mindfulness of faith. They include media, music, movies, devotions, biographies, screenplays, concordances, devotionals, books, and the list goes on. When we listen intently, view with discernment and give understanding to the things that may catch our interest, our faith is being developed in ways we cannot even imagine. Taking God at His word is designed to release His goodness to transform our life. We must be careful what we decide to let in our temple. 1Corinthians 6:19 says, "Know ye not that your body is the temple of the Holy Ghost which is in you, which ye have of God, and ye are not your own?"

Figuring out what you believe about Jesus is a huge decision, and it should not be taken lightly. Your faith in Jesus seals who you are in Him and the kingdom of God. Following Jesus is a journey, and it takes great faith to withstand the things we will go through. "The Lord hath prepared his throne in the heavens; and His kingdom rules over all" (Psalm 103:19). Heaven is His throne; He sits enthroned in all the glory of His majesty, with all His attendants. The overall purpose of Psalm 103 is to show that He reigns, rules, and governs over all things.

The ultimate faith we aspire to have in God thoroughly ties into what we hope for and what we must do (actions) to attain it. For example, if a cake recipe requires 3 ½ cups of cake flour to ensure the cake rises to the expected perfection along with all the other ingredients, and if we eliminate an ingredient by accident and only put in 3 cups (leaving ½ cup out), then we cannot expect the same results. Our faith is to believe and trust for an expected outcome of the awaited results that we are believing God for.

In 2021, I personally prayed to have more money in my bank account. I asked the Lord if I should go back to work part-time to have extra cash in my account or to put my faith in gear and believe God for a miracle for it. Genesis 12:2 says, "And I will make of thee a great nation, and I will bless thee, and make thy name great; and thou shalt be a blessing." When we believe for His miraculous favor on our lives and believe that He is a rewarder to those who diligently seek Him, He shows us miracles. (Hebrews 11:6). God's timing is not our timing, and please know that the Lord did not answer immediately. The supernatural instructions I received in my spirit in order to receive the money I was believing and petitioning for before God was to do what the Holy Spirit instructed me to do. The Holy Spirit instructed me to look inside my closet in a dusty, heavy metal box that I kept important documents in. So, inside the metal box were paper statements from working as a state appointed employee in past years. I then placed a phone call to the retirement system and inquired about a refund/direct deposit authorization form to get back the time I had invested when I worked for the state. I was then informed over the phone of how much I was entitled to receive back, and it surprised me in a very pleasant way.

Clearly, I became ecstatic with joy about how my faith had hoped for something I could not see. Jesus literally taught me what the true acronym for FAITH is: I *Found Assurance in Trusting Him* when I needed it most! I spoke it, I received instruction from God, He confirmed it by the action required on my part to believe, and He honored it. When we believe and do our part, which requires action, we shall receive the blessing when it is God's will.

The Kingdom of God is a progressive revelation to many. Everything in the kingdom is appropriated by faith. "For there is the righteousness of God revealed from faith to faith; as it is written, The Just Shall Live by Faith" (Romans 1:17). This kind of multi-dimensional faith caused me to speak and have the money I needed in my bank account. We do not know how everything is going to work out, but we must have enough faith to believe for it to work out according to the faith we have within us.

Sharing this experience with you is by no means to boast; it is only a testament to the development of my faith. My sole purpose is to be transparent, to edify, and to encourage others. I have accepted the call to be a disciple for the Lord Jesus Christ. Writing this book truly has blessed and enabled me to share with others the actions I have taken that may be helpful to many. Philippians 2:4 (ESV) says, "Let each of you look not only to his own interests, but also to the interests of others." God knows we all need to be encouraged. 1 Thessalonians 5:11 says, "Encourage one another and build each other up." Also, in Proverbs 12:25, it says, "Anxiety weighs down the heart, but a kind word cheers it up."

Our faith has many dimensions. Faith brings the unseen into the visible world. Hebrews 11:39-40 says, "God has a better promise for us, and all these having been attested through their faith, did not receive the promise. God having provided something better for us, in order that they should not be perfected apart from us." Ephesians 5:13 says, "But everything exposed by the Light becomes visible in its time and season." For everything that is illuminated becomes light; a light in and of itself. 1 John 1:5 states, "God is light and in Him is no darkness at all." Habakkuk 2:4 states, "See, the enemy is puffed up, his desires are not upright, but the just shall live by faith."

Luke 17:5-8 states, "The apostles said to the Lord, 'Increase our faith!' And the Lord said, 'If you had faith like a grain of mustard seed, you could say to this mulberry tree, 'Be uprooted and planted in the sea,' and it would obey you. Suppose one of you has a servant plowing or looking after the sheep. Will he say to the servant when he comes in from the field, 'Come along now and sit down to eat'? Won't he rather say, 'Prepare my supper, get yourself ready and wait on me while I eat and drink; after that you may eat and drink'?"

The above scripture references demonstrate that exercising and increasing your faith can determine what your faith accomplishes. What we persist in and do repeatedly becomes easier for us to realize the more we do it. It has been given to serve you. When you establish the right relationship with your faith, you will experience what Romans 4:17 says: "By faith, we call those things which be not as though they were." This spiritual confidence settles that everything physical becomes obvious. For example, God created light by calling for "light" when only darkness was there.

The new covenant description means we can go directly to God through Christ. Hebrews 7:22 (NIV) states, "Because of this oath, Jesus has become the guarantee of a better covenant." There is forgiveness of sins only through the new covenant. It is the communion and walking in the Holy Spirit, therefore, which revitalizes a sinner with new life. It depicts the radical change of the sinner and his new relationship to Jesus Christ living within us. Isaiah 66:1 says, "Heaven is my throne, and the earth is my footstool." When we place our feet on what Jesus defeated on the cross, the earth becomes our footstool. As Jesus Christ says in John 19:30, "It is finished." These last words from Christ clearly say how He paid the debt owed to His Father, and it was wiped away, paid in full. To be honest, Jesus eliminated the debt owed by mankind – the debt of sin. Continually place your feet on what Jesus Christ defeated on the cross for us.

"God who has called you into fellowship with His Son Jesus Christ our Lord, is faithful." 1 Corinthians 1:9. Also, Matthew 9:29 says, "Then Jesus touched their eyes and said, "According to your faith will it be done to you."

"Listen to your heart"

REFLECTIONS

REFLECTIONS

2

How to Develop Faith

Developing faith comes by seeing it as it happens. The more we experience our faith accomplishments, the greater our faith is elevated. Our understanding process becomes favorable because we have witnessed the experience with our actions when we wait on the expected return. As we dive into the many ways to develop our faith, let's be mindful that our steps are being ordered and that by following the leading of Christ, you will know what is the best way. The objective is to develop greater depths of our observations in seeking to develop our passions. The areas listed below prayerfully will equip us to gain an understanding of the values to be applied in our lives concerning faith.

My Prayer: "Holy Spirit, we thank you in advance for teaching us how to develop the kind of faith needed for the equipping of your people. Enable us to do the task. Help us to gain an understanding of why and how it happens as you open our minds to pick up and learn what you want us to know concerning each item listed. Help us to develop innovative solutions by your Spirit to resolve issues we may encounter along the way. Our goals are to follow your lead as well as your instructions to become more astute and to propel the learning process to your advantage. In Jesus' name I pray, Amen."

After God has called you to do an assignment, He will then equip you to do the task. He will also qualify you to do the work, and the enablement comes from the Holy Spirit. The Apostle Paul wrote, "I am sure of this, that He who began a good work in you will bring it to completion at the day of Jesus Christ" (Phil 1:6). So, no matter what, that WORK is in you that God placed in your heart. He can empower you to do it, but it must be for His glory and His glory alone.

Listed below are vital aspects to focus on when developing your faith. Every topic will be briefly touched upon:

- Grow in the Love of God
- Repent from Your Old Lifestyle
- Receive God's Word
- Study to Show Thyself Approved unto God
- Believe His Word
- Meditate on His Word
- Cross Reference Scriptures with Other Scriptures
- Listen for His Voice
- Trust God
- Apply the Word to Your Life
- Pray for Others
- Listen to God & Do What He Asks of You
- When it Gets Hard, Do Not Quit

- Often Reflect on Past Faith Blessings
- Stir up Your Gifts
- Encourage Yourself & Others
- Surrender to God's Will
- Be Courageous
- Speak God's Word
- Set Aside Time to Hear God's Voice
- Decree & Declare

1. ***Grow in the Love of God*** – It is dynamic to grow in the love of God. Agape love shows we are filled with the fullness of God (Ephesians 3:19).

2. ***Repent from your Old Lifestyle*** – Our new mind sees things God's way instead of our own, and we experience transformation.

3. ***Receive God's Word*** – God's Word directs us to wisdom. Psalm 119:130 says, "The unfolding of your words gives light; it gives understanding to the simple."

4. ***Study to Show Thyself Approved unto God*** – Put forth every effort in teaching every word accurately. Do not misapply God's Word (2 Timothy 2:15).

5. ***Believe His Word*** – It not only provides an entity of faith, but it gives us a basis to believe God, which is unshakeable faith.

6. ***Meditate on His Word*** – Think deeply about what God has said to you.

7.   *Cross Reference Scriptures with Other Scriptures* – When we let scripture interpret scripture, it gives us another context and explains what we are reading.

8.   *Listen For His Voice* – We get to know Him in a more intimate way, and we hear what He is saying to us.

9.   *Trust God* – He knows what is best for our life better than we do. His track record is perfect, and He has proven Himself faithful. When we apply the Word of God to our life, we experience His blessings (Proverbs 3:5).

10. *Pray For Others* – Praying for others changes us. "The effectual fervent prayer of a righteous man avails much" (James 5:16).

11. *Listen to God and Do What He Asks of You* Because He knows all things, we gain new perspective (Numbers 30:31).

12. *When it Gets Hard, Do Not Quit* – Walk it out because going through tough times builds character, and faith never quits.

13. *Often Reflect on Past Faith Blessings* – Reflection causes us to slow down, it reminds us how He has brought us through, and it recaps our priorities.

14. *Stir Up Your Gift(s)* – Your gift will make room for you in the world and enable you to follow your

dreams. "For God has not given us a spirit of fear but of power, love and self-control" (2 Timothy 1:7).

15.   *Encourage Others* – It causes others to enjoy being around us (Hebrews 10:24-25).

16.   *Surrender to God's Will* – Philippians 2:6-8 shows us that Christ was willing to surrender His rights as the second person of the Trinity to the will of the Father. So, we must surrender our will to God.

17.   *Be Courageous* – Deuteronomy 31:7: "Be strong and courageous, do not be afraid or tremble at them for the Lord your God goes with you. He will not fail or forsake you."

18.   *Speak God's Word* – Hebrews 4:12: "For the word of God is alive and active. Sharper than any double-edged sword, it penetrates even to dividing soul and spirit, joint and marrow; it judges the thoughts and attitudes of the heart."

19.   *Set Aside Quiet Time to Hear God's Voice* – Calendar quiet time to hear God's voice.

This list on how to develop faith can also be used as affirmations in developing stronger faith. All topics can also be used as daily devotions. When we know them to be true in our life, they are confirmed when we decree and declare them out loud. As we speak them aloud, our faith is speaking what it believes. Believing always comes before seeing.

20. *Decree & Declare* – What does it mean to decree and declare a matter? To decree is to issue an authoritative command and to declare means to state (out loud) a fact. Is it biblical to declare? Yes. God's Word has power and authority when we see these principles as His word.

Faith Acts

When you speak out loud, in doing so, it is a corresponding action.

Corresponding action – Luke 17:12-19
Faith can be seen through actions – Read Luke 5:17-20
We have been justified through faith – Romans 5:1

REFLECTIONS

REFLECTIONS

3

Do You Have Great or Little Faith?

Walking in obedience unto God is the walk of faith because you do not know where He is leading you. "Faith is being sure of what we hope for and certain of what we do not see" (Hebrews 11:1). Undoubtedly, in most cases, it leads to a place where you have never been, and God's objective is for you to trust Him. The scripture that comes to mind is Proverbs 3:5, which says, "Trust in the Lord with all your heart and lean not unto your own understanding; in all your ways acknowledge Him and He shall direct your paths." God's sovereignty is to be acknowledged in all that we do and think. In the end, God will get all the glory and honor that belongs to Him.

When these types of experiences occur in our life, both great and little faith, it is settled. However, as we grow in Christ, we begin to see His perspective from a clearer vantage point, for example in James 2:18, "Someone will say, 'You have faith, I have deeds.' Show me your faith without deeds, and I will show you my faith by what I do."

I believe we've all experienced these types of incidences to say the least by doing what Jesus asks us to do for Him. This kind of trust in Jesus undeniably declares a confidence and a trust that only He can develop in us. "He who trusts in the Lord will prosper" (Proverbs 28:25). I have personally learned that man will fail you, but God will never fail you. Anyone who trusts God will never be put to shame. These Bible stories contain wisdom for our life.

Great faith was demonstrated by **The Woman with the Issue of Blood** in Mark 5:25-34, "Who bled for twelve years. She suffered many things by many physicians, and had spent all that she had, and was nothing bettered, but rather grew worse. When she had heard of Jesus, she came in the press behind, and touched His garment. For she said, 'If I may touch but His clothes, I shall be whole.' And straight away the fountain of her blood was dried up; and she felt it in her body that she was healed of that plague. And Jesus, immediately knowing in Himself that virtue had gone out of Him, turned Him about in the press, and said, 'Who touched My clothes?' And His disciples said unto Him, 'Thou sees the multitude thronging thee, and sayest thou, Who touched me?' And He looked round about to see her that had done this thing. But the woman fearing and trembling, knowing what was done in her, came and fell down before Him, and told Him all the truth. And He said unto her, 'Daughter, thy faith hath made thee whole; go in peace, and be whole of thy plague.'"

Great Faith of a Canaanite Woman – Mathew 15:21-28

"Leaving that place, Jesus withdrew to the region of Tyre, and Sidon. A Canaanite woman from that vicinity came to him, crying out, 'Lord, Son of David, have mercy on me! My daughter is demon-possessed and suffering terribly.' Jesus did not answer a word. So, his disciples came to Him and urged Him, 'Send her away, for she keeps crying out after us.' He answered, 'I was sent only to the lost sheep of Israel.' The woman came and knelt before Him. 'Lord, help me!' she said. He replied, 'It is not right to take the children's bread and toss it to the dogs.' 'Yes, it is, Lord,' she said. 'Even the dogs eat the crumbs that fall from their master's table.' Then Jesus said to her, 'Woman, you have great faith! Your request is granted.' And her daughter was healed at that moment."

The Faith of the Roman officer – Matthew 8:5-13

"'Lord,' he said, 'my servant lies at home paralyzed, suffering terribly.' Jesus said to him, 'Shall I come and heal him?' The centurion replied, 'Lord, I do not deserve to have you come under my roof. But just say the word, and my servant will be healed. For I am a man under authority, with soldiers under me. I tell this one, 'Go,' and he goes; and that one, 'Come,' and he comes. I say to my servant, 'Do this,' and he does it.' When Jesus heard this, he was amazed and said to those following him, 'Truly I tell you, I have not found anyone in Israel with such great faith. I say to you that many will come from the east and the west, and will take their places at the feast with Abraham, Isaac, and Jacob in the kingdom of heaven. But the subjects of the kingdom will be thrown outside, into the darkness, where there will be weeping and gnashing of teeth.' Then Jesus said to the centurion, 'Go! Let it be done just as you believed it would.' And his servant was healed."

Faith of the Men who had Leprosy – Luke 17:12-19

"As He was going into a village, ten men who had leprosy met him. They stood at a distance and called out in a loud voice, 'Jesus, Master, have pity on us!' When he saw them, he said, 'Go, show yourselves to the priests.' And as they went, they were cleansed. One of them, when he saw he was healed, came back, praising God in a loud voice. He threw himself at Jesus' feet and thanked him, and he was a Samaritan. Jesus asked, 'Were not all ten cleansed? Where are the other nine? Has no one returned to give praise to God except this foreigner?' Then he said to him, 'Rise and go; your faith has made you well.'

Little Faith

Matthew 16:8 – "Which when Jesus perceived he said unto them, 'Oh ye of little faith, why reason among yourselves because ye have brought no bread?'" Jesus reminded the Pharisees and Sadducees of the five loaves, of the five thousand it fed and how many baskets were taken up afterward. Neither did they remember the seven loaves of the four thousand, and how many baskets they took up they took up then. Jesus asked the question in Matthew 16:11, "How is it that ye do not understand that I spake it not to you concerning bread, that ye should be aware of the leaven of the Pharisees and of the Sadducees?"

Jesus rebuked the wind because his disciples were fearful of drowning. Matthew 8:23-27 – "And when he entered in to a ship, his disciples followed him. And behold, there arose a great tempest in the sea, insomuch that the ship was covered with the waves: but Jesus was asleep. Awakened by the disciples, Jesus got up and rebuked the wind and the raging waves. So, they ceased, and there was a calm."

The only one who can measure great faith versus little or no faith at all is God. Keep on believing God's Word. Never be misguided away from it by what you see. Many in the Bible were not ones with great faith when they first started out in their faith walk but attained great faith through the correction of God.

God's Words of Life on Faith
"Everyone born of God overcomes the world. This is the victory that has overcome the world, even our faith."
1 John 5:4

"Though you have not seen Christ, you love him; and even though you do not see him now, you believe in him and are called with an inexpressible and glorious joy, for you are receiving the goal to your faith, the salvation of your souls."
1 Peter 1:8

REFLECTIONS

REFLECTIONS

4

Meditate on God's Word

Meditating on God's Word is vital. It not only tells you what His promises are, but it gives you guidance for your life. As you better understand God's word, you will be reassured that you are never alone. Also, when we delight in His word and draw near to Him, He draws near to us. We begin to learn how He intimately wants us to trust Him even when we go through difficulties in our life. His word comforts us, it guides us, it builds our confidence, and He pours out the love He has for us through the leading of the Holy Spirit. When we meditate, it reminds us of His protection and love for mankind. Also, when we serve a loving God like this, how can we not want to develop a relationship with Him? This kind of love is not foretold anywhere but in the Bible, which is unprecedented.

When we worry, God tells us not to in His word and why. There are times we may feel hopeless, but God speaks of His statutes concerning the areas we will all face in this life.

God's tool to develop the necessary skills we need is for us to set aside quiet time to meditate. Our reading is the attribute He wants us to receive to be a blessing toward others. God's ability to bundle such a beautiful gift is to show His love. The wonderment of this gift clearly demonstrates John 3:16 – "For God so loved the world that he gave his only begotten son that everyone who believes in him shall not perish but have eternal life." In Ephesians 5:2 it says, "Walk in the way of love, just as Christ loved us and gave up His life for us as a fragrant offering and sacrifice to God." When we know what love is, then we want to express love.

When we read God's word, our minds are being transformed into His way of thinking, and when we do not take the time to read or meditate, our minds are infused with the things of the world. Sometimes we can become overtaken with worldly imaginations, infractions, and ungodly insights. Romans 12:2 says, "Do not be conformed to this world, but be transformed by the renewal of your mind, that by testing you may discern what is the will of God, what is good and acceptable and perfect." When we mimic the things of this world, we can easily become carnal and of the world. God's Word will infiltrate our entire being to walk in His ways. Human logic will fail you, but walking in the Spirit and acknowledging God is walking in the light. Whoever lives by the truth comes into the light, so that it may be seen plainly that what they have done has been done in the sight of God (John 3:21).

We all rightfully know how life can and does get extremely busy at times with genuine things that we must do, but when we are living on purpose and add self-control and discipline by meditating on God's Word, it will keep us from being ineffective and unproductive. Sometimes we must challenge ourselves to do so, but when we do, we reap the benefits and it is pleasing unto God.

The benefits of meditating on God's word also include that we become more knowledgeable of His Word, we learn how the Old and New Testament principles tie right into our lives, and we see how love covers a multitude of sins. We learn the importance of having patience in our life and that the Golden Rule is to do unto others as you would have them do unto you. Meditating clears our mind and calms us. Worrying about things is simply not trusting. To take God at his word is to select a passage or a scripture you would like to think on deeply. Intentionally setting aside time and quietness to meditate on the word is essential in developing a more intimate relationship with Him. As you meditate, you can often ask yourself questions about the content, then ponder what you have come up with. This application process causes you to invoke or summon thought processes to dig even deeper into meditating and to learn more about the word.

Meditation creates the mental space to study, and it takes practice to remain focused, so do not become discouraged if you get off track. Take a break, then refocus because the enemy will distract you in any way he can to prevent you from attaining knowledge about the word. In John 10:10 it says, "The thief comes only to steal, kill, and destroy; I have come that they may have life and have it to the full."

When we pray before we meditate, we should ask the Father to give us His grace to master this practice as we discipline ourselves and spend quiet time with Him. Remain hopeful to hear what the Holy Spirit is specifically saying to you. Let the Bible grow your faith, mind, and soul. Question – When you read the Bible, do you apply it to your life? Meditation on God's word is applying it to your heart. It involves thinking, asking, and praying. As David prayed in Psalm 104 – Let my meditation be pleasing to you, God.

God's commandments in Psalm 119:97-105 make us wise. His words are "A lamp to my feet and a light to my path." Also, the word will empower you, and it will have a personal effect on your heart and your life. It simply guides you towards thinking about His word and praying to Him. Meditation is where we get refreshed just like Jesus did when He went alone to pray. In Mark 1:35, He felt that it was necessary to be alone with God. When you do the same, God will speak to your heart, give you direction for your life, and help you to live it out in the strongest way. He is an intimate, personal being who loves you. He is also willing to give you direction and instruction for your life when you let Him.

Listed below are just a few of the benefits we receive when we meditate:

- Our spirit is quieted and calmed.
- Our mind is enlightened.
- It increases our energy.
- Your heart is purified.

- Your capacity of loving God is enflamed.
- He will show you what is in your heart.
- You will have increased love for Him.
- Your faith will skyrocket.

"Whether you turn to the right or to the left, your ears will hear a voice behind you, saying, 'This is the way; walk in it.'" Isaiah 30:21

REFLECTIONS

REFLECTIONS

5

Quintessential

The meaning of quintessential is representing the perfect example of a class or quality. As we grow in the knowledge of Christ and develop our faith, we must represent Christ in powerful and impactful ways (See Philippians 1:6). Also, the Apostle Peter said who we are in Christ. In 1 Peter 2:9 it says, "But you are a chosen race, a royal priesthood, a holy nation, a people for His own possession, that you may proclaim the excellencies of Him who called you out of darkness into his marvelous light." When we literally take God at His word, our faith will make us whole, and His power is available to us when we apply it.

The root of the matter is the essential heart of an issue. For example, when our faith is released and it takes root as what we are believing for, we must do our part to put it into corresponding action by speaking words that generate activity to produce the manifestations we seek. When we release our words into the atmosphere by speaking them, it activates positive results and God honors our faith life. Words are powerful. Life and death are in the power of the tongue, according to Proverbs 18:21. When we value our words and believe they will come to pass, we should be watchful about what we say. The power of the tongue must always be scrutinized. Proverbs 10:19 says, "In the multitude of words sin is not lacking, but he who restrains his lips is wise."

King David is a perfect example of a quintessential person in the Bible. Many of his actions were quality representations of who he was in Christ, and he was a man after God's own heart. He did not want to appeal to mankind. He was not mindful of man's approval of him, nor did it matter. David's yearning was to follow God at all costs. He was strong in battle, he was bold, and he trusted the Father for the protection of his life. His faith did not require being intimidated because he saw fit to please his judge (God). He also fought Goliath with stones. This kind of faith does not need to be built up to increase it. Jesus is the seed of King David, and so are we. John 7:42 says, "Hath not the scripture said, That Christ cometh of the seed of David, and out of the town of Bethlehem, where David was?" David was the first King God elected and chose. He was an accomplished musician that the Lord had selected. Also, he defeated eternal enemies and crushed the Philistines as he was appointed by God.

Jesus Christ is quintessential, and He too demonstrated it throughout the Bible. He was all about His Father's business. In Luke 2:49, He told his earthly parents, "Why did you seek Me? Did you not know that I must be about My Father's business?"

Luke 7:22 – "Jesus answered and said to them, 'Go and tell John the things you have seen and heard: that the blind can see, the lame can walk, the lepers are cleansed, the deaf hear, the dead are raised, and the poor have the gospel preached to them.'"

2 Timothy 2:4 – "No one serving as a soldier gets entangled in civilian affairs, but rather tries to please his commanding officer. Remember, that Jesus Christ, the seed of David, was raised from the dead according to my gospel, for which

I am being chained like a criminal. But God's word is not chained."

1 John 5:1-4 – "Whoever believes that Jesus is the Christ is born of God, and everyone who loves Him loves his child as well. This is how we know that we love the children of God: by loving God and carrying out His commandments.
In fact, this is love for God: to keep His commands and those commands are not burdensome, for everyone born of God overcomes the world."

Joseph was measured as the righteous one. His brothers thought that his father loved him more than any of them, and they detested him. Joseph had a dream and told his brothers, which made them dislike him even more. In a nutshell, as they were binding sheaves of grain, which is a harvesting process, Joseph told his brothers about the second dream and how his sheaves stood upright but his brothers' grain bowed down. The brothers thought the meaning of the dream was that Joseph would reign over them. So, his brothers became jealous of him.

As I accelerate this story along, Joseph's brothers sold him after they stripped him of his robe and threw him into a cistern. They disowned Joseph and convinced their father that he was dead. In Genesis 50:19-20, Joseph said to them, "But as for you, you meant evil against me; but God meant it for good." The golden rule is to "do unto others as you would have them to do unto you." This demonstration is a virtue of being kind, and it is a gift. Joseph could have easily become overly enraged when he finally met up with his brothers even after being put in prison, but he did not. Joseph showed brotherly love and compassion toward them.

When we choose to do the right thing, we become more like Christ, and our faith is a necessity to reach our destiny. Train your spirit with faith words, not doubt. What you say is what you get. The words we positively speak change the atmosphere. Luke 17:5-6 shows us that even a little faith is very powerful.

Mankind was made to rule the earth. Genesis 1:26-28 **says,** "And God said, let us make man in our image, according to our likeness; and let them have dominion over the fish of the sea and over the birds of heaven and over the cattle and over all the earth and over every creeping thing that creeps upon the earth. And God created man in His own image; in the image of God, He created the male and female. And God blessed them; and God said to them, be fruitful and multiply, and fill the earth and subdue it, and have dominion over the fish of the sea and over the birds of heaven and over every living thing that moves upon the earth."

REFLECTIONS

REFLECTIONS

6

The Voice of God

The voice of God can be heard by the reading of His Word, audibly, through his prophets and apostles, through dreams and visions, by hearing graceful impressions within your entire being, by listening to a donkey, or by any means God chooses. John 10:27 says, "My sheep listen to my voice, I know them and they follow me."

I have personally heard the voice of God audibly at a perilous time in my life and when I needed to hear from Him. My life had progressively become frantic, and I honestly did not know what to do or how to bring about a resolution to my problem. I believe God was teaching me how to quiet myself down so that I could be more attentive, listen to His voice, and make a necessary decision which was crucial on my part instead of worrying about the matter. I was increasingly pressed on every side and somewhat reluctant to come to a decision. The extreme mounting pressure resulted in me literally calming myself down and praying from my heart. I then began to listen intently to hear what God would say to me. I then heard God's voice say to me audibly,

"Listen to your heart," and His voice was crystal clear. In Ezekiel 3:10 it says, "Moreover, He said to me, "Son of man, take into your heart all My words which I will speak to you and listen closely." God's word never returns to Him void.

I remember hearing God's voice as if I heard it yesterday. This experience, accompanied by no one other than God, totally changed my life on this side of heaven. In Ezekiel 43:2, the prophet proclaims God's "voice was like the sound of many waters" (see Revelation 1:15). I empathically share the same viewpoint because when I heard God's voice it precisely sounded just like the sound of many waters. Hearing God's audible voice is a desired experience for many as it was for me then, and there will always be a longing in my heart to hear his voice again on this side of heaven audibly. God's voice has echoed in my spirit on several occasions for years.

God Encounters – The word "encounter" means to "run into," and running into God is the greatest experience that can happen to us! God Encounters are not about a one-time dramatic experience but an unending leading of the Holy Spirit operating in our lives. Encounters with God can propel you into your destiny and endow you with incredible favor to proceed confidently in daring exploits for God's kingdom and to attain marvelous access to places you've never thought of or imagined.

The book you are currently reading is the first time I've intentionally shared my experience in book form. Remarkably so, this God encounter has transformed my life forever. I am learning to share these experiences more openly and freely with others by taking the limits off God's ability to do what He does best, which is to perform miracles in the lives of His people.

God encounters will openly be shared with others as I continue to live this earthly life and as the Holy Spirit leads me. This experience has increased my faith to an all-time high. The more I share about the God encounters I've experienced, I realize it not only pleases the Father but also those who follow Him. My belief is that it's God's desire for us to encourage and inspire others to set the captives free. "Stand fast therefore in the liberty wherewith Christ hath made us free, and be not entangled again with the yoke of bondage" (Galatians 5:1 KJV).

After every ending in doing so (setting the captives free), our actions can become the brightest horizon of our next phase of a beautiful life as well as establishing a closer relationship with God. Also, we stand firm and do not let ourselves be burdened again by a yoke of slavery. My question to you after reading the above two God encounters that I've shared is this, and please ponder your response before the Father: "Will you also rise to the occasion to set captives free?" When we openheartedly welcome the fact that God knows the best way to speak to us individually and to rightfully get our attention, we respond to His will and not our own. Speaking freely allows us to be delivered from the ways of this world's rationality and to boldly walk confidently into the freedom of God encounters that He wants us to embrace and experience in this life.

My disposition to share my personal experiences with you is also to demonstrate my total dependence upon Jesus in my life. This book is to also encourage others and myself to be available for God to use as His vessel, to remove confusion from our minds, and to help us be led by the Spirit of God. He will endow us with liberty and empower our willingness to be revolutionary people for His Kingdom—if we let Him. He will also cause many to have a total disregard for the things of this world, to set our mind on things above, and not on earthly things (Colossians 3:2).

God will enable us to decrease controversial disputes (especially when we can reference scripture based on His ability to talk to us in the Old and New Testament).

I believe we can become more equipped to become tenacious about God's Word and know why so many are perplexed about His nature. The Bible clearly says in Isaiah 55:8, "My thoughts are not your thoughts, neither are your ways my ways," declares the Lord. The truth of the matter is, God is smarter than us! Psalm 147:5, Psalm 139:4, and Psalm 139:1-24 teach that His ways appear to be unbelievable to mankind, but they are not to God. So, let us look at more scriptures to raise our faith level based on the Word of God because He is very capable to do far more than we can ever think or imagine (Ephesians 3:20).

The second time I heard God's audible voice was when I was dealing with another difficulty in my life, and God said audibly to me, "Look at Paul." At first, I thought God was referring to my now deceased husband's life because his name was Paul and he frequently ran from the calling God had on his life. There was just something about commitment to the Lord that made my then husband Paul feel very uncomfortable. The running and chasing chronicle I discovered was strictly between the two of them. At times in our lives, God will intimately deal with us about what is required on our part to do His will. Sometimes we tend to brush it off and ignore the expected accountability of what is required on our part, and often we may think we can run from the matter as if we didn't hear what God said. "The eyes of the Lord are everywhere, keeping watch on the wicked and the good" (Proverbs 15:3).

In the Bible it also says that God is omnipotent. God spoke creation into existence (read Genesis 1). God being omnipotent to me means that He has unlimited power and can do anything. He didn't just shape what we can see visually;

God created things that didn't even exist until He spoke it into existence. My question to you now is, "Who can outrun God?" My response is "NOBODY." What is your response?

So, I started reading about the Apostle Paul in the New Testament to get a better understanding of what I needed to learn. Afterward, the revelation came to me about Paul in the Bible, and I clutched onto the revelation. I began to see the importance of in-depth reading about the story of Paul in the Bible. God revealed to me that He was referring to the Apostle Paul in the Bible. God wanted me to read the Word – the Bible, His word (W.O.R.D.) = Acronym – Without Reading Diligently, how will you know Me? Subsequently, I started reading about the life of Saul/Paul. Paul persecuted Christians at first, but then he was personally taught by Jesus Christ.

The trials and tribulations of life at times can become very perplexing—at least for me they have from time to time. Bewildering aspects coupled with frequent trials can become overwhelming in our minds to the degree that our antenna (frequency) is not quite tuned in (like an untuned radio station producing static) with the Holy Spirit. Furthermore, those that we love dearly cannot give us the right advice or counsel to make a meaningful and impactful witness to our spirit, especially if they have never been in the same or a similar dilemma. Nonetheless, because I had no one to reach out to about my circumstance, I first prayed to the Lord. Secondly, I needed to hear God's perspective on the matter by reading His Word, and thirdly I read about the Apostle Paul in the Bible, which allowed me to direct my focus on the Word of God, His peace, and how to conquer what I was dealing with at that time. Once I became more focused, God's grace and His peace overshadowed everything I was dealing with, and I was delivered and set free by hearing His voice. John 8:32 says, "Then you will know the truth, and the truth will set you free."

God's Audible Voice
(Biblical Scriptures Referencing God's Voice)

"He fell to the ground and heard a voice say to him, 'Saul, Saul, why do you persecute me?' 'Who are You, Lord?' Saul asked. 'I am Jesus, whom you are persecuting.' He replied. 'Now get up and go into the city, and you will be told what you must do.' The men travelling with Saul stood there speechless; they heard the sound but did not see anyone. Saul got up from the ground, but when he opened his eyes, he could see nothing. For three days he was blind, and did not eat or drink anything" (Acts 9:4-9).

"Then the man and his wife heard the voice of the Lord God walking in the garden in the breeze of the day, and they hid themselves from the presence of the Lord God among the trees of the garden. But the Lord God called out to the man, 'Where are you?'…'I heard Your voice in the garden,' he replied, 'and I was afraid because I was naked; so, I hid myself' (Genesis 3:8-9).

Matthew 12:18 – "And a voice from heaven said, 'Behold my servant, whom I have chosen; my beloved, in whom my soul is well pleased: I will put my Spirit upon him and he shall show judgement to the Gentiles.'"

Isaiah 6:8 – "Then I heard the voice of the Lord saying, 'Whom shall I send? And who will go for us?' And I said, 'Here am I. Send me!'"

2 Peter 1:17-18 – "He received honor and glory from God the Father when the voice came to him from the Majestic Glory, saying, 'This is my Son, whom I love; with him I am well pleased.' We ourselves heard this voice that came from heaven when we were with him on the sacred mountain."

When we make ourselves available to God, He will avail Himself to us.

Build Your House on the Rock

Faith Can Move Mountains

Matthew 17:20
"He replied, 'Because you have so little faith. Truly I tell You, if you have faith as small as a mustard seed, you can say to this mountain, 'Move from here to there' and it will move. Nothing will be impossible for you.'" If our faith is like a mustard seed, it is enough to move mountains, and by faith many in the Bible have done surprising things, and we too can remove mountain like problems.

REFLECTIONS

REFLECTIONS

7
Psalm 37

Do not fret because of those who are evil or be envious of those who do wrong; for like the grass they will soon wither, like green plants they will soon die away. Trust in the Lord and do good; dwell in the land and enjoy safe pasture. Take delight in the Lord, and He will give you the desires of your heart. Commit your way to the Lord; trust in Him and He will do this: He will make your righteous reward shine like the dawn, and vindication like the noonday sun. Be still before the Lord and wait patiently for Him; do not fret when people succeed in their ways, when they carry out their wicked ways, when they carry out their wicked schemes.

Refrain from anger and turn from wrath; do not fret – it only leads to evil. For those who are evil will be destroyed, but those who hope in the Lord will inherit the land. A little while, and the wicked will be no more; though you look for them, they will not be found. But the meek will inherit the land and enjoy peace and prosperity. The wicked plot against the righteous and gnash their teeth at them; but the Lord laughs at the wicked, for he knows their day is coming.

My Footnote

King David wrote Psalm 37, and he gives us insight of how we are to place ourselves in a position not to fight the enemy but to rest in the Lord because God will fight our battles for us. When we place our trust in the Lord and take delight in Him, He has prepared a righteous reward for us. Exhausting our energy on the wicked one who is already defeated in God's eyes is simply wasted time and energy. When we refrain from anger and do not allow vengeance to take root in us, we are trusting what God's word says, and God is pleased with our non-reactionary outcomes. This world we live in is a temporary dwelling place; we are just passing through and we must be mindful to wait for the glory that is before us. Think about it: fighting battles is exhausting and can take us into a psychological zone of defeat both physically and mentally. However, we need to realize the wicked one was already overpowered by our Lord when He died on the cross for us and was resurrected so that we may live with Him in paradise.

Also, because the wicked one knows that he is already a conquered foe, he taunts us to make us think he wins, but it is not so. When our righteous ways shine like the dawn, the brightness of God's glory burns like coals of fire in the enemy's nostrils. The more we take delight in the Lord, the more the wicked one opposes us, but to God belongs all the glory. Opposition is not comfortable for anyone; nevertheless, when we realize who fights our battles for us, we also have a knowing in the spirit that victory will win its finest battle.

Hostility and unfriendliness will always surface when we stand up against an opposing force (the enemy). We are instructed to refrain from anger, to turn from wrath, and to not fret over it. Wickedness turns to evil which is morally shameful and sinful. An evil transgression causes pain, injury; it is harmful and morally wrong. These purposefully inflicted actions upon many are premeditated sin and are willful defiance against God.

Psalm 37 clearly instructs us to not agonize over it as they will soon have their day. I believe we've all come against various forms of opposition in our life, but it builds character in our life and we become stronger individuals in our faith walk. We are overcomers. 1 John 5:4-5 says, "For everyone born of God conquers the world. This is the victory that has overcome the world, even our faith. Who is it that overcomes the world? Only the one who believes that Jesus is the son of God."

The word of God in Romans 12:21 says, "Do not be overcome with evil, but overcome evil with good." Life has a way of pressing many buttons, and we may want to get back or take revenge for the evil that has been done to us. When we attempt to take things into our own control, a whirlwind of wrongdoings on our part is revealed in our actions which would rightfully be displeasing to God. However; when we do not allow vengeance to take its direction in our life, we then begin to see how it all unfolds when we let go and let God. Is this easy to do? No, but it can take root in us to regulate our own actions and surrender to let His perfect will be done in our life. We must believe that He will settle the disobedience taken against us in His timing.

Nonetheless, when we attempt to take matters into our own hands and try to make God relinquish His way of solving the matter, we can hypothetically interrupt things according to God's perfect will for the outcome. When we hope in the Lord and keep His ways, He will exalt us to inherit the land, and when the wicked are destroyed, you will see it. The Lord helps them and delivers them; He delivers them from the wicked and saves them, because they take refuge in Him. Taking refuge in God despite what others may say or do to us is the best place we can be as contenders because God knows the beginning and the end.

Vengeance is not a place for us to chase after because God considers the blameless and observes the upright; a future awaits those who seek peace. Blessed are the peacemakers, for they shall be called the sons of God. "For whoever desires to love life and see good days, let him keep his tongue from evil and his lips from speaking deceit; let him turn away from evil and do good; let him seek peace and pursue it" (1 Peter 3:10-11 ESV).

"The salvation of the righteous is of the Lord: He is their strength in the time of trouble. And the Lord shall help them, and deliver them: He shall deliver them from the wicked, and save them, because they trust in Him" (Psalm 37:39-40).

In a nutshell, the noonday sun shines brighter and brighter as the day progresses. As we allow our righteousness to not engage in fighting our own battles, let us take God at His word. Take delight in the Lord, and He will give us the desires of our heart (Psalm 37:4 NIV).

John 1:15 (NCV)
"The Light shines in the darkness, and the darkness has
not overpowered it."

REFLECTIONS

REFLECTIONS

8

Words

Words are used as an expression when we communicate ourselves to others, when we write, and when God communicates to us in the Bible or however He sees fit. The words we speak change the atmosphere. In the beginning, God used words to unlock the dialog for the entire world, inspiring people to participate and learn of Him, to read, and to hear external words in various languages about Him all over the world. Words are used to express who God is, to capitalize on His exceptional pathway to unfold creation, and to unfold to mankind who He is and how the world came into existence. The way He expresses himself as creator of heaven and earth has many scratching their heads. His disclosure of authentication clearly is unprecedented and puts Him in an extraordinary class all by Himself. Translating the Bible is a never-ending process as well, as the process of communicating it accurately has been undertaken by multitudes of Bible scholars old and new. They are challenged continually and have been for centuries.

Consequently, the power of words when spoken and written is indispensable when communicating to another. Many express their feelings by writing in a journal, notebook, or elsewhere when inspired. However, when inspired by God, ensure that you are saying what He wants you to say. He knows that we are imperfect individuals because He made us, and we can do nothing without His help, so we must strive to be the best ambassador we can be on His behalf if we are to be a representative for Him. Many were inspired by the Holy Spirit in writing the Old and New Testament.

Genesis 1:1-3 says, "In the beginning God created the heavens and the earth. Now the earth was formless and empty, darkness was over the surface of the deep, and the Spirit of God was hovering over the waters. And God said, 'Let there be light,' and there was light." When God spoke the above-mentioned words, He saw that the light was good, and He separated the light from the darkness. God called the light "day" and the darkness He called "night." And there was evening and "night," and there was the morning of the first day.

As we continue to read on in Genesis 1, we learn also how God continued to speak and said, "Let us make mankind in our image, in our likeness, so they may rule over the fish in the sea and the birds in the sky, over the livestock and all the wild animals, over all the creatures that move along the ground." Speaking words into existence is a force that expedites our faith into the things we cannot see but still hope for. When our faith is developing, He requires that we trust His will and believe that He will give us what his child requires.

I have learned and continue to learn that the things that I speak are vital. God is seeking to teach us the way of faith. Real moral fiber is developed by disciplined faith. Faith does not happen overnight; it takes time and patience, and it is strengthened over time through trial and sometimes error. Keep on believing God no matter what you think or feel. Never give up on God, because He will never give up on you.

The words we speak about a particular situation can ruin the outcome if we are not mindful of the negativity when negative words surround it. Faith speaks what it believes even if we cannot see it. If we can see it, it's not faith. Remaining hopeful about matters concerning the desires of our heart ultimately perpetuates an intensity for our faith to be increased and even rise to higher levels no matter what it looks like. I'm confident you have overheard the cliché, "Be careful what you ask for because you just might get it." I speak these words because I've seen it happen in my own personal life, and you can too. The words we use can translate into a negative impact as well as a positive impact.

As we learn the importance of our words when expressing ourselves when praying and communicating, we begin to see a pattern of God's blessings and His goodness in our life. The scripture says, "You have not because you ask not" (James 4:2). The core of this verse is simple: we do not have because we do not ask for it. Mark 11:24 clearly says, "Therefore I say unto you, what things soever ye desire, when ye pray, **believe** that ye receive them, and ye shall have them."

When I began to apply this foundational principal to my own life, I then saw things change for the better according to God's will and purpose for my life. I had the blessings, and my desire is to see you have them as well.

Also, when we begin to take on the things of what Jesus did for example, as Jesus said in John 14:12-14, "Very truly I tell you, whoever believes in Me will do the works I have been doing, and they will do even greater things than these, because I am going to the Father. And I will do whatever you ask in my name, so that the Father may be glorified in the Son. You may ask me for anything in my name, and I will do it" (John 14:14 NIV).

Because Jesus said it and He cannot lie, He means it.
When we take our faith to higher levels, we begin to see manifestations in our life to empower us. We also see miraculous empowerment on others. As we aspire to encourage other believers and even those who do not have a relationship with Christ, Jesus is awakening us. Also, when we encourage others to increase their faith and for others to just believe, it is based on our testimonies that we share, and it also inspires them to share their experiences with others.

Speaking and calling those things that be not as though they were, doing exploits for God and His Kingdom, and being transformed to the destiny to which you have been called will encourage more of God's people to live through being disciples for Christ.

Adding to our experiences in this life through our destiny is growth. They are not just for us alone, but for others as well. None of us were put on an island all by ourselves to live this journey called life alone.

As we begin to pray more, ask for the desires of our heart, trust God more, and believe that what we pray for will come in God's perfect timing, we must take all the time limits off. God is in control, not us. Remain steadfast and patiently wait for what He has promised you. God's faithfulness will overtake you. God knows when you need the blessing. I can honestly say I am a witness to God's goodness in my life. Speaking what we believe is like the invisible oxygen we breathe in daily. There is no other like God! We must position ourselves to just believe. We all must experience God on our own, and my prayer is that you let Him in your life to show you personally how much He loves you. In Jesus name I pray, Amen.

WORDS

∧

Without Reading Diligently, How Will You Know Me?

REFLECTIONS

REFLECTIONS

9
Living by Faith

A vast number of us live to accomplish our career goals by obtaining degrees from accredited colleges (as well as some colleges that claim to be accredited and we find out later they never were). To be successful in a career that we love and where we see ourselves, we must be dedicated, self-motivated, and faith-driven to attain our goals. The path we often take is relentless despite everything else that it may involve—all to enjoy the finer things in life. Subconsciously, with much added stress, our dreams may include the following: travelling, purchasing a dream car, going back to school, the repayment of student-loans, working full & part-time jobs, paying a mortgage, and raising a family.

The goals that we factor in are coupled with experiencing and living a better life; when it's all said and done, one may find it very difficult to justify the subliminal underlying measures it will take to objectively pursue and sustain a life of being tenacious to accomplish those goals. The motivation it takes to endure and sustain this life sometimes takes a whole lot more than just going to a gym to exercise and release this type of suppressed stress. However, it can come from living and practicing a disciplined life of divine faith. Also, our readiness to accomplish our goals can sometimes lead to added pressures from loved ones, peers, and society. When we focus on what others think about striving to succeed in this life, we can sometimes lose focus. Yet, when we place more emphasis on living by faith and believe that God will help us with our goals, nothing becomes impossible with Him if we believe.

There have been times when I have pursued avenues in my own life which I thought were tailor-made just for me, and I ended up going in the direction of being in hot pursuit only to find out later that it was a skill that was essential for me only to learn a life lesson to apply subsequently in life and not necessarily immediately. As mentioned, it was not a wrong avenue to pursue, but it led to creating other possibilities to employ in my life and to add substance to my character that I believe God was developing in me.

Living by faith is a daily practice we learn. Think about it: before we became Christians, we relied heavily on our own capability and intelligence, and those actions only took us so far and not any further.

Noah had to believe God for rain. I am a witness that living by faith does not always make sense to us (as well as to others). Can you fathom how Noah built an ark when he had never been in rain? Go figure. Talk about your faith shifting while waiting on the promise. It can change your entire perspective, it can give you the tenacity to hold on, and it can give you the endurance to believe when a final gas bill comes in the mailbox before the actual check you were waiting for is hand delivered to you. Nevertheless, our actions of waiting calmly and still believing in the process strengthen and increase our ability to remain and live by faith. When insurmountable curveballs come our way, faith must always remain as our confidence in trusting God.

As we continue to live by faith, we become more aware of what it means to stand in opposition despite what we are going through. The Holy Spirit has the ability to bring back things to our remembrance of past situations we have dealt with in the height of facing opposition, and the ability to realize and see victory must be overcome by the blood of the lamb. When we use our faith, I believe God is pleased with us. Also, when we truly trust the Father, we are literally living in the freedom of God. Consequently, we must use repellent which is the Word of God to get rid of the weeds and twigs in our own garden (our life). This action is also called spiritual warfare. As we are more aware of our potential for growth in this area, we must do our part to keep the soil worthy for seeds to be planted in and use the necessary positives for continued growth.

Weeds that are grown from previously established roots, can become dormant, which are an offset of continued hindrances to growth. Yet life does not stop because of unwanted weeds; they grow regularly and eventually crack and break easily. So, my question to you is, "What necessary steps are you taking to live a life of faith?" If you have not taken any steps already or you simply do not know what steps to take to live a life of faith, it's never too late to start a list and live by what you believe to be true to yourself and God. When we live by faith, we are also mandating an intimacy for our faith walk with Him. Discipline is key, and it requires work.

Effective people develop self-purpose in their lives. When it is personalized, written down, and looked at frequently, It will help us to reach our goals and to hopefully not derail from our purpose even when life gets tough. Setting big goals in our life will eventually produce stepping stones of advancements and accomplished triumphs which will allow us to hold on to the successes that we pleasantly welcome. Journaling is a creative tool I enjoy. I can recall writing down my own thoughts in journals for years. I currently still do because I like to pick them back up to re-read them at different times and seasons in my life. I regularly become amazed at God's faithfulness and goodness in my life. To literally revisit deep-rooted journal entries is very inspirational to see where you came from and to reflect on your spiritual growth or incomplete goals. I have frequently looked in old journals over the years and have been astonished at where I was during various periods in my life, only to be inspired by the faith developed or even the things I fell short of.

Habakkuk 2:2 says, "Write the vision and make it plain upon the tables, that He may run that readeth it." Journaling helps us remember what the vision is. Furthermore, it is a practical measuring instrument we can use to continue believing for the things we cannot see as it inspires us as well as others and proves how faithful God is in our lives. As we live by faith, we also learn by faith.

Learning by faith requires the following: mental, spiritual, and physical energy. Mentally, one must be focused and determined to climb the peaks and walk in the valleys when journeying through our faith walk. Even if we lose heart, as it can sometimes occur, and even when we are more hard pressed than we can ever think or imagine, our faith walk takes time to develop as it matures continually. Our faith base is determined to get us through it all and enable us to conquer what is placed before us. The scripture that comes to mind is Philippians 4:13 – "I can do all things through Christ who strengthens me." The physical exertion requires us to develop stamina so that it allows us to be strengthened so we do not become weak while going through struggles. In Nehemiah 8:10, we read that His joy is our strength (and not our own).

Spiritually, if we do not know God's word, how will we be able to fight the good fight of faith? God's word needs to be known by us and easily communicated through us so that whenever the enemy throws a dagger our way we will know how to fight back with God's word. We must be prepared to speak the Word of God at a moment's notice. When we know what to do in life as well as what we have learned from God, we live by faith and apply it when we act. Living by faith is the substance of what we believe. He died on a cross for us, and that salvation is what He is doing now in our lives and what He will do in the future. His death and resurrection are our foundation for life. The Word of God that we feed on determines the direction of our life and faith.

The faith I continue to ascertain on daily basis in my life is a direct result of the following:

- Read God's Word.
- Keep believing no matter what it looks like.
- Believe for the unbelievable because God is faithful.
- Seek His will for your life.
- Take the time limits off as to when God is going to make it happen.
- Trust God wholeheartedly.
- Make and take time to quiet yourself to hear Him speak to you.
- Share God's goodness with others.
- Let your faith develop and increase more as you learn to trust Him and experience life.
- When instructed to do His will, just do it.
- Remember that you are never alone—He is always with you.
- Gain experience by doing, listening, applying, and demonstrating.
- Be aware of life's involvements and the knowledge of thought processes.
- The belief of a result becomes an answered prayer.
- The intense aspect of achieving one's desired results from God is to appreciate His faithfulness.
- Thank God in advance before the breakthrough even happens.
- Know that God's light will shine upon achieved outcomes.
- Turn your desired motivations into witnessed results.
- Stand on this scripture: Matthew 7:7 "Ask, and it shall be given unto you; seek, and you will find, knock, and the door shall be opened unto you" (NIV).
- Be strong even when the situation appears bleak.

- Know that God hears your cries when difficulty arises, remain strong, and keep your faith built up as it's preparation for a blessing.
- Encourage yourself when necessary.
- The points of reference which result in the choices of resources are obtained through God's guidance.
- Be thankful and cultivate the many blessings you've received in your life.
- When you close your eyes at night, know that you are loved by God and highly favored.
- Be and become a blessing to others, as those qualities awaken your gratefulness.
- Let your light shine for the glory of God.

Joshua 1:3 says, "Every place which the sole of your feet treads, I have given it to you, just as I spoke to Moses."

REFLECTIONS

REFLECTIONS

10

Trials and Tribulations

It's a fact that we will all face trials, tribulations, persecutions, and sufferings in life. However, our faith must require action. "By faith we understand that the universe was formed at God's command, so that what is seen was not made from what was visible. By faith Abel brought God a better offering than Cain did. By faith he was commended as righteous, when God spoke well of his offerings, and by faith Abel still speaks, even though he is dead. By faith Enoch was taken from this life, so that he did not experience death: He could not be found, because God had taken him away. Before he was taken, he was commended as one who pleased God. And without faith it is impossible to please God, because anyone who comes to Him must believe that He exists and that He rewards those who earnestly seek Him" (Hebrews 11:3-6).

"By faith Noah, when warned about things not yet seen, in holy fear built an ark to save his family. By his faith he condemned the world and became heir of the righteousness that is in keeping with faith. By faith Abraham, when called to go to a place he would later receive as his inheritance, obeyed, and went even though he did not know where he was going" (Hebrews 11:7-8).

Many of the above faith actions are found in Hebrews 11: 1-8, and faith was required of them. Faith was demonstrated by all of them and ongoing through verses 9-38. You may ask yourself, were they all tested and had to go through trials and tribulations? The answer is yes, and we too are also tested and must endure until the end. God wants us to endure hardship as a disciple. God is treating you and I as His children because we are (Hebrews 12:7). "What children are not disciplined by their father?" If you are not disciplined, and everyone undergoes discipline, then you are not legitimate, not true sons and daughters at all. As we respect our earthly fathers for disciplining us, we must also submit to our heavenly Father and respect Him. God disciplines us for our own good, in order that we may share in His holiness. No discipline seems pleasant at the time, but painful. Later, it produces a harvest of righteousness and peace for those who have been trained by it" (Hebrews 12:11 NIV).

A gem cannot be polished without friction, nor a man perfected without trials. James 1:2-6 says, "Consider it pure joy, my brothers, and sisters, whenever you face trials of many kinds, because you know that the testing of your faith produces perseverance." Frankly speaking, I do not think I have ever considered it pure joy when I was going through a trial, but please do not judge me because I am still a WIP: work in process. "Let perseverance finish its work so that you may be mature and complete, not lacking anything" (James 1:4). If you are asking the question – "Why must we face trials and tribulations?" Listed below are some of the reasons why we face trials:

1. Trials help us to build our faith in God.
2. We learn to trust God more.
3. We become overcomers.
4. Trials test our faith.
5. Tribulation humbles us.
6. Trials & tribulations are inevitable.
7. Trials help us to persevere.
8. Adversity develops character.
9. Tribulation opens doors.
10. They remind us of who we are in Christ.
11. They remind us that we are never alone.
12. We experience breakthroughs & deliverance.
13. We realize that the Lord is our helper.
14. Trials encourage us to pray.
15. They makes us realize how much we should rely on God.
16. Trials let us share in His sufferings.
17. They allow us to help another in a similar situation.
18. We receive a greater reward in heaven.
19. They show us the sin in our lives.
20. They remind us that God is in control.
21. Trials help us learn God's Word.
22. They increase our knowledge.
23. They teach us to be more thankful.
24. Trials encourage us to talk more to God.
25. They allows us to experience His grace and mercy.
26. Tribulation increases our faith.
27. Trails convict our heart.

28. Tribulation makes us repent.
29. We become bold and confident in Christ.
30. We become less worldly.
31. We are more grateful.
32. Trials stop us from complaining.
33. They convict us when we are not patient.
34. They encourage us to believe.
35. They remind us when we are not content.
36. They convict us to lay our burdens down.
37. They convict our hearts if we are not spending time with God.
38. Trials nudge us to act.

Sometimes we suffer trials and tribulations because of our own mistakes and because we follow the wrong voice. When we decide to take matters in our own hands and not follow God's will, we must suffer through the choices we make.

The word of God says in Psalm 34:19, "Many are the afflictions of the righteous, but the Lord delivers him from them all." Personally, I have lost count of the trials, and I for one am just keeping it real.

James 1:4-8 says, "Let perseverance finish its work so that you may be mature and complete, not lacking anything. If any of you lacks wisdom you should ask God, who gives generously to all without finding fault, and it will be given to you. But when you ask, you must believe and not doubt, because he who doubts is like a wave of the sea, blown and tossed by the wind. That person should not expect to receive anything from the Lord. Such a person is double-minded and unstable in all they do." When we endure suffering for Jesus' sake, we can usually hold up under the intense pressures of life because Jesus helps us and we are literally standing on what Christ has already done. God will never quit on us.

Genesis 9:13

"I set my bow in the cloud, and it shall be a sign of a covenant between Me and the earth."

REFLECTIONS

REFLECTIONS

11

Speaking the Word of God

Faith believes, and then faith speaks according to what it believes. Think about it again: God spoke creation into the universe, and it happened. When we speak out loud what we believe by speaking His word and believe in our heart without doubting, we begin to see the miraculous happen. The power of the spoken word of God, when spoken in faith in the name of Jesus, has great power to overcome speechless and undefeatable obstacles in a believer's life. This is why it's so important to speak the word of God as it has great power. God's word when spoken will not return void to Him (Isaiah 55:11). We were created in the image of God; therefore, we must say and learn how to articulate out loud what we are believing God for. If we do not know the promises of God, we must study to say what He says. One of God's promises is found in Psalm 89:34: "No, I will not break my covenant; I will not take back one word of what I said." The promises of God are yes and amen. 2 Corinthians 1:20 says,

"For all the promises of God in Him are Yes, and in Him Amen, to the glory of God through us."

When we study to learn God's promises as His own people, we must believe them in our heart and speak them out loud. Believing and speaking God's will over our life is mandated by His will from the beginning. I dare you to try it, then watch what happens. God cannot lie; He is faithful and will prove his faithfulness to those who believe. When you take God at his word, He will perform it. There have been many times that I've personally experienced God's timeliness and practicality in my own life. The one thing I can emphasize most is that when exercising faith, we need to remove all time constraints. Just keep on believing until your prayer is answered and wait for your prayer to manifest or be answered. God's timing is not ours. His will and purpose for it to happen solely depends on how He sees fit in making the blessing appear in one's life because He is in control. On numerous occasions, the blessings happen when we least expect them, but they are memorable answers and reminders to our prayers when they do happen. Faith believes and speaks what God has spoken. When He speaks, we must trust what He has revealed, no matter how incredible it seems. Because God is in the business of performing extraordinary things in our life to His glory, it requires us to believe and not doubt. I have believed for many things in my life, and as I am a witness, I encourage you to trust Him. God can do it, and He is faithful.

When we set a boundary or limit the capacity of what God can do in our life by not studying His word, speaking His promises out loud with our mouth, and patiently waiting on the blessings, we miss out on truly experiencing the abundance as well as God's goodness to be shared with others. This kind of confidence is developed over time, and practicing our faith requires action. When faith speaks what it believes, we trust God even more in the seen and felt dominion. In the kingdom realm where God is, He can demonstrate and showcase things we have never even thought of or imagined; that's how powerful God is. Since this type of trust is required, I believe it takes a relentless confidence inside us to do what is required of us so that God can show up and show out. I cannot express enough how Bible faith creates and requires action.

What we declare by faith already exists. It takes the invisible and brings it into the seen realm. When we see the Bible as a divine force given by God, we must emanate Him. Jesus set the example for us to use our faith to bring to pass those things that we cannot see.

The more we start speaking out loud what we believe, the more we will see God manifesting our prayers right before our very own eyes. If I have not already said the foundational principles for these blessings in your life, they are to trust the Father, speak His Word out loud, and continue to pray until it happens. These kinds of blessings do not happen by coincidence, but they already exist when we take God at His word (the Bible). The word of God is a powerful force when we speak what He has already spoken. Since His promises have already been spoken, our faith in action activates those promises in our life. Faith without works is dead, so spring forth by speaking His words with your mouth.

Engage your mouth and tongue with God's word to build up your faith. If we do not build our faith by doing what it takes to see His promises, we will become stagnant and become bewildered because we are not experiencing our full potential of spiritual growth. The word of God is in our heart and in our mouth. Out of his heart flows the issues of life (Proverbs 4:23). "As a man thinketh, so is he." What you say flows from what is inside of your heart.

Read Proverbs 23:7. The Bible kind of faith is not speechless; it speaks what it believes, and if you do not have faith in God, you will not speak it. On the other hand, in Mark 11:14, Jesus spoke to the fruitless fig tree and said, "May no one ever eat your fruit again!" Sure enough, what He said happened: the fig tree withered and died. The examples Jesus demonstrated for us through His Word (the Bible) should also be demonstrated by us with our mouth. Having trust evokes action, and Faith speaks what it believes.

What Christ did at Calvary for both you and I was triumphant, and His actions clearly demonstrated His love for us. Therefore, we must demonstrate our love for Jesus by speaking the word of God. It is not a strange thing to go through persecutions or trials because the trial of your faith is you being tested to see if you have sufficient faith.

2 Corinthians 4:13-14 says, "It is written: 'I believed; therefore I have spoken.' Since we have that same spirit of faith,

we also believe and therefore speak, because we know that the one who raised the Lord Jesus Christ from the dead will also raise us with Jesus and present us with you to Himself."

Declaring what you already know to be true is speaking it out loud. We all have human reactions of the things we've gone through in life; however, looking back on past experiences should also remind us all that we are never alone, and God confirms this in His Word by reassuring us that He will never leave or forsake us (Deuteronomy 31:8). Jesus is enough for everything that we go through in life, and He goes before you. In God's Word it shows us the distinction between a revitalizing tongue and a destructive one. "Death and life are in the power of the tongue, and those who love it will eat its fruit" (Proverbs 18:21). Therefore, when going through life be careful what you say out loud.

Believe that you have received God's promise and speak it. Speak God's promises daily in faith. "It is written: 'I believed; therefore, I have spoken.' Since we have that same spirit of faith, we also believe and therefore speak" (2 Corinthians 4:13).

You may ask the question, what does God think about tall trees? In Genesis 2:9 trees are "pleasing to the eye." Trees are essential to human life, and God's Word makes us strong like the tree of life. Proverbs 3:18 says, "She is a tree of life to them that lay hold upon her: and happy is everyone that retaineth her."

REFLECTIONS

REFLECTIONS

12
Decree & Declare

When we decree a matter over our life, revelation knowledge freely flows within us so that we can release our faith and joy in the atmosphere. You ask the question, "is there a difference between decreeing and declaring? The answer is yes. To decree is to command by a verdict while to declare is to make clear, explain, or interpret. The definition of decree is an official order issued by a legal authority.

In Psalm 2:7-12 NIV it says, "I will proclaim the Lord's decree: He said to me, 'You are my son, today I have become your father. Ask me, and I will make the nations your inheritance, the ends of the earth your possession. You will break them with a rod of iron; you will dash them to pieces like pottery.' Therefore, you kings, be wise; be warned, you rulers of the earth. Serve the Lord with fear and celebrate His rule with trembling. Kiss His son, or He will be angry and your way will lead to destruction, for His wrath can flare up in a moment. Blessed are all who take refuge in Him." After reading Psalm 2 (all of it, I must add), I discovered that if you carefully read those verses, you can undoubtedly see that to decree a thing is the part of what God said.

The psalmist then delights in the law of the Lord by declaring (explaining) the decree. In God's Word (the Bible) it says in Job 22:28, "Thou shalt also decree a thing, and it shall be established unto thee: and the light shall shine upon thy ways" (King James Bible). If God already said it, then it is a decree; however, we can declare it by explaining and making it clear. This process illustrates basically how powerful and life changing God's word is when we read the Bible line upon line and precept upon precept and then put it to practical application.

This type of freedom in the spirit cleanses the layers of impurities we unknowingly have, but God knows, and He can divinely deliver us. If you want to receive the promises of God, decree it and then declare it. Never hold back, as that is what the enemy wants you to do: doubt God. If you believe you have received increase, unconditional love, favor, humility, or wealth, then go ahead and decree God's blessings in these areas of your life. Declare them and you will have them. If you want God's fulfillment of your heart's desire or even want to have God's goodness and favor in your life (they too are all promises), you can decree blessings on your life by saying them out loud. God has given us these tools in His Word (the Bible). Only speak the Word of God and you will have it when you declare it.

Having complete dependency on God galvanizes our complete trust. If you are already a believer, then you already know that God is faithful. The answer may not come when we want it, but He is always right on time. God's timing is perfect in every aspect of our lives when we believe what He has already said. We can even decree that Jesus sits on the throne of our heart. Do you believe it? If you do believe it, then decree it out loud and watch what God does (keep in mind, His timing is perfect).

Our faith is tested as pure gold. The trials of our faith will bring praise, glory, and honor to the King of Kings when we totally rely on Him in every area of our life.

We are called to believe in the one who sent Jesus (John 6:28-29). That is the work we are called to do. Believing in Jesus is our work. When Jesus is revealed in our life, God is glorified.

The proclamation of decreeing blessings on your life as well as the lives of others will revolutionize you. You will begin to see things change in your life, your faith will increase, and you will see God's hand move in many situations that will totally amaze you in His timing. The increase of divine blessings will overtake you. When you decree God's Word, you are literally saying what He has already said. God does not lie. God confirms His word in John 6:63, "The words I speak unto you, they are spirit, and they are life." God's word is full of life and is very powerful. Try using His words for yourself; you will not be disappointed. Dig deep in the Word to show yourself approved and find out what His promises are throughout the entire Bible. God is speaking to us, but sometimes we just do not take the time to read. Excuses will get us every time, and what happens? We just miss out!

God wants us to step into a new lifestyle of learning. "Do not be conformed to this world but be transformed by the renewing of your mind" (Romans 12:2). When our minds are renewed, we begin to experience innovative creativeness when He speaks through His word, and reading it helps us to develop a genius mindset that He created. To follow His lead and to listen will bring about the development required to hear what He is saying. God wants to improve and develop our lives. When God speaks to you, listen to what is being said. Word inspired utterances in faith will create many blessings in our life; however, if not spoken, it will not take place. God has placed the creative authority of words in our mouth. Many times, God will point us in another direction and pathways to follow His lead to remove our own. When we become unfulfilled in our lives, we can ask the Lord to increase our faith, and He will. In Luke 17:6, He says, "If you had faith as small as a mustard seed, you could say to this mulberry tree, be rooted up and planted into the sea and it will obey you."

When we listen attentively to the switch, we are in the will of God and not our own. Miracles and divine outpouring of God's Spirit become even more tangible for the desires of heart that we have longed for to happen. Again, doing something different manifests God's blessings. He created both you and I in His image, so He will protect you and empower us with His wisdom. If doing something different is a requirement on your part and it came from the throne of

God, just do it! We will have no regrets and we will live to share it with others who were at one time in their lives being in control of their own will (self-independence) rather than being in complete dependency of God. We owe it to ourselves to adopt the lifestyle of totally being reliant on God.

Seriously, if we did not depend on God, we would die. We are nothing without Him. Our physical and spiritual relationship is solely dependent upon Him. Depend means to place reliance and trust on God instead of ourselves. When we have complete dependence on Him, we see and let His will be done in our lives, and it is better than we can ever imagine it to be, and we will not miss out on the great things He has planned for us who love Him. Stay connected to God and again speak the word (decree it, declare it) and begin to see what He will do for you. His surprises will overtake you, and you will know without a shadow of a doubt that God's love is unconditional and unending. We are truly loved by Him. He wants the best for us.

John 6:28-29 – "Then they said to Him, 'What must we do, to be doing the works of God?' Jesus answered them, 'This is the work of God, that you believe in Him whom He has sent.'" It is our faith work when we believe in whom He has sent.

In conclusion, "Believing Faith Speaks" is a true testament of how Kim Thompson the author allows her own faith to be increased and enriched as she continues to witness and see the spiritual experiences in her own life that she now writes and speaks about to many. This development and the growth of believing and speaking those things that be not as though they were is called faith. I have recognized and witnessed revolutionary lifestyle phenomena happen when one sincerely trusts the Lord Jesus Christ because He is faithful.

"Let's us unwaveringly increase the faith we profess, for He who promised is faithful" (Hebrews 10:23).

If you take the time to increase your faith and continually do so, then stand back and watch the breakthroughs of God's goodness and endless astonishments happen in your life.

REFLECTIONS

REFLECTIONS

Acknowledgements/ Contributions

Michael Thompson (but he goes by Tee) is my best friend, my husband, the love of my life, and the person who makes the best potato salad on the face of this earth. God put us together for such a time as this. I am overwhelmed with joy that you were selected by God for me. Surely, the Lord picked His best when you came into my life. I want to personally thank you for believing in me and being the senior editor for *Is Your Faith Ready for An Uplift?* When I asked you to be an editor for the book, you willingly jumped in to assist with the process, and you were not apprehensive to put yourself out there, even having never done this type of editing. Also, your assistance in the project made the difference when it came to fine tuning the final draft. Thank you again for helping to get it published. I love you.

Ms. Peggy Williams, our angel on this side of heaven. When I came to Winston-Salem, NC, and met you for the first time, your contagious smile put me at ease, and it allowed me to rest in the Lord. Thank you for allowing both Tee and I to stay at the Hope House for him to heal and recover from his injuries. God's grace, love, and compassion was evident in every way as we stayed there for four months until

Tee recovered from his injury. Also, thank you for volunteering to help as being an editor for this book, God's book. I would also like to thank Pastor Sandra Ireson and all the members at Pine Grove United Methodist Church for your prayers and for being God sent warriors in our eyes.

Mr. Stanley & Sue Morgan, your willingness to go the extra mile in doing what you do is priceless. We watched as you both took it upon yourselves to ensure that everything at the Hope House was supplied for. It was remarkable to witness and to hear of your many years of service and dedication. You both ensured the living quarters was clean, the pantry and refrigerator were stocked, and even the landscaping was maintained and taken care of during our stay. Also, when we saw Stan's intuitiveness to ensure that a ramp be built for easier access inside/outside at the Hope House, we remained hopeful and happy to be placed amongst great individuals of your caliber. Thank you.

About the Author

 Kim Thompson is from Santa Monica, California, but now happily resides on the East Coast. She enjoys writing, cooking, and baking. Traveling abroad is an all-time favorite for Kim and her soulmate. Retirement is a welcomed addition to her new lifestyle which enables her to write and publish more books and to decree the goodness of God to others. The Holy Spirit's guidance, coupled with developing steadfast faith, continues to grow as she shares with others to encourage those who seek to grow their intimacy with God through the books she writes.

As the Holy Spirit continues to instruct and lead more specifically, she follows Habakkuk 2:2 NLT – "Then the Lord said to me, 'Write my answer plainly on tablets, so that a runner can carry the correct message to others.'"